Cyber security fundamentals 1

Learn your internet role

Md Tapon Mahamud Jony
12/5/2020

Abstract

Do you know a hacker can access your real life from your virtual life data! Now a day's data breach is one of the common words from small to multinational companies. Now days, many companies spent billions of dollars only to protect their private or public data. From this book you will able to learn what could be your role while you are entering to the internet world and protect yourself from the different types of hacker who are waiting for your small tiny mistakes.

This book will give you an overview of how to protect your devices, creating strong passwords and safely using wireless networks. It also discusses maintaining your data securely. Your online data is worth something to cyber criminals. This book covers authentication techniques to help you maintain your data securely. It also covers ways to enhance the security of your online data with tips about what to do and what not to do online.

Table of Contents

1. Chapter One
   - 1.1 Cybersecurity Definition..6
   - 1.2 3P's Measure..7-8
   - 1.3 CIA Triad..8
     - 1.3.1 Confidentiality...9
     - 1.3.2 Integrity..10
     - 1.3.3 Availability..10-11
   - 1.4 Common Security Vulnerabilities..11
     - 1.4.1 Software Vulnerabilities...12
     - 1.4.2 Hardware Vulnerabilities...13-14

2. Chapter Two
   - 2.1 What is Malware..14
   - 2.2 Types of Malware..15
     - 2.2.1 Spyware..16
     - 2.2.2 Adware...16
     - 2.2.3 Bot..16
     - 2.2.4 Ransomware..17
     - 2.2.5 Scareware...17
     - 2.2.6 Rootkit..17
     - 2.2.7 Virus...18
     - 2.2.8 Trojahorse..18
     - 2.2.9 Worms..19
     - 2.2.10 Man in the Middle...19
     - 2.2.11 Man in the Mobile...19
   - 2.3 Symptoms of Malware..20
   - 2.4 How does Malware infected your computer................................20-21

3. Chapter Three
    3.1 Data Privacy and Protection..22
        3.1.1   Protect your computing devices..........................23
        3.1.2   Keep the fire wall on..23
        3.1.3   Use Antivirus software...24
        3.1.4   Protecting your devices....................................24-25
        3.1.5   Wireless network safety....................................25-27

4. Chapter Four
    4.1 Social Engineering..28-29
        4.1.1   Social Engineering Calls..29
        4.1.2   In-Person...29
        4.1.3   Online...30
    4.2 Common Attacks Technique...30
        4.2.1   Pretexting...30
        4.2.2   Tailgating..30
        4.2.3   Something for Something.....................................31
        4.2.4   Wifi Password Cracking...31
        4.2.5   Social Engineering..31
        4.2.6   Brute-force attacks...32
        4.2.7   Network sniffing..32
        4.2.8   Phishing..32
        4.2.9   DDos..33
        4.2.10 SEO Poisoning...34
    4.3 What is Impact Reduction..35-36
    4.4 How to Prevent Social Engineering....................................37
        4.4.1   Keep software and computer updated................37

  4.4.2 Think twice before clicking on links..................................37

  4.4.3 Don't trust free software..38

  4.4.4 Backup your data..38

  4.4.5 Use security software..38

  4.4.6 Protecting your computing devices...............................39

  4.4.7 Firewall Manage..39

  4.4.8 Use Antivirus and antispyware......................................39

  4.4.9 Manage your operating system.....................................40

  4.4.10 Protect all your devices...40-41

  4.4.11 Use unique passwords...42

  4.4.12 Good password tips..42

  4.4.13 Encrypt your data...42-43

  4.4.14 Social Media Sharing..44

  4.4.15 Phishing calls & emails...45-47

 4.5 Email and Web Browser Privacy...47-48

 4.6 Best Security Practices..49-51

 4.7 IDS and IPS..51-52

 4.8 Mobile Phone Security..52-54

5. Chapter Five

 5.1 Contingency Plan..54

 5.2 IT Contingency Planning...55-56

 5.3 Virtual Private Network (VPN)...57

 5.4 Concluding speech..57

6. References...58-60

Chapter One

1.1 Cyber Security Definition

Cyber security is the practice of defending your computer systems, IT network, and applications against the digital attacks. These cyber-attacks are usually aimed at accessing, obtaining, or destroying sensitive information.

They might try to extort money, steal your personal data, or interrupt your normal business activity.

Learning about digital security and how to execute powerful measures is especially testing today since innovation is continually advancing and cybercriminals are getting progressively creative.

Figure 1: Security Prototype Sample

1.2 3P's measure

We have to remember 3P's to measure cyber security terms to remember cyber security tree.

Figure 2: 3P's Measure

People - You must understand and comply with basic data security principles like choosing strong passwords, being wary of email attachments, and backing up data.

Policy - Organizations must have policies for how they deal with both attempted and successful cyber-attacks. These should explain how you can identify attacks, protect systems, detect and report threats, and recover from successful attacks.

Protection - Technology is vital to giving institutions and individuals the computer security tools needed to guard themselves from cyber-attacks. Modern technologies used to defend against cyber-attack include firewalls, malware safety, antivirus software, and email security filtering.

A proactive cyber security technique has multiple layers of protection spread throughout the computers, networks, programs, or statistics that you intend to hold safe. In an organization, the people

policy, and safety must all complement each other to create a powerful defence powerful protection from cybercriminals. Cyber Security Facts According to the study conducted by the University of Maryland, there is a hacking attack in every 39 seconds. There are millions and millions of data breaches every single year. According to Juniper Research, the total data breach will exceed $150 million. Most of the cyber security attacks are in small businesses. Therefore, if you are a small business owner, you need to take proper care of it. Guess what? More than 90% of the errors are due to human mistakes. Only a few percentages of the attacks are using automated tools. Others are due to human mistakes.

1.3 What is the CIA triad?

The *CIA triad* is a widely used information security model that can guide an organization's efforts and policies aimed at keeping its data secure.

The model has nothing to do with the U.S. Central Intelligence Agency; rather, the initials stand for the three principles on which infosec rests:

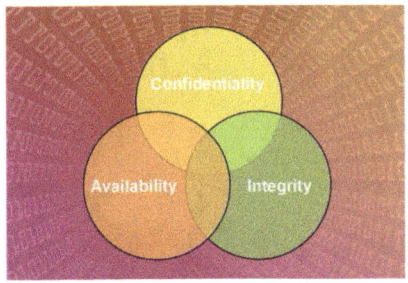

Figure 3: CIA Triad

1.3.1 Confidentiality

Only authorized users and processes should be able to access or modify data guarantees that sensitive records are accessed handiest with the aid of an authorized character and kept far from the ones not legal to own them.

It is applied the usage of safety mechanisms together with usernames, passwords, access manage lists (ACLs), and encryption. It is also common for records to be categorized consistent with the volume of damage that would be done ought to it fall into unintentional hands. Security measures can then be implemented accordingly.

1.3.2 Integrity

Data should be maintained in a correct state and nobody should be able to improperly modify it, either accidentally or maliciously. Integrity guarantees that statistics are in a format that is genuine and correct to its authentic purposes. The receiver of the statistics ought to have the statistics the creator meant him to have. The statistics can be edited via authorized persons handiest and remains in its authentic state whilst at rest. Integrity is applied the usage of protection mechanism consisting of information encryption and hashing. Note that the adjustments in statistics can also occur as a result of non-human-brought on occasions inclusive of an electromagnetic pulse (EMP) or server crash, so it's critical to have the backup system and redundant structures in area to ensure statistics integrity.

1.3.3 Availability:

Authorized users should be able to access data whenever they need to do so. Availability ensures that statistics and resources are to be had to the ones who want them. It is applied the use of methods such as hardware maintenance, software program patching and network optimization. Processes inclusive redundancy, failover, RAID and high availability clusters are used to mitigate serious effects while hardware troubles do occur. Dedicated hardware gadgets can be used to defend towards downtime and unreachable facts due to the malicious action which include disbursed denial of service (DDoS) attacks.

1.4 Common Security Vulnerabilities

Security vulnerabilities are any sort of programming or hardware deformity. In the wake of picking up information on vulnerability, malicious clients endeavour to exploit it. An exploit is the term used to portray a program written to exploit a known weakness. The objective of the attack is to gain access of a system framework, the information it has or to a particular assets of host.

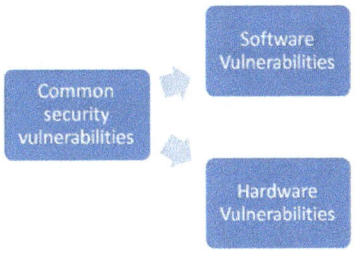

Figure 4: Security Vulnerabilities Process

1.4.1 Software vulnerabilities

In general, software vulnerabilities are introduced by errors in the operating system or program code, given all the attempts made by organizations to identify and fix vulnerabilities in software, new vulnerabilities are popular to emerge. Application updates are also common. Applications such as web browsers, mobile apps and web servers are often updated by the companies or organizations responsible for them. In 2015, a major vulnerability, called SYNful Knock, was discovered in Cisco IOS. This vulnerability allowed attackers to gain control of enterprise-grade routers, such as the legacy Cisco 1841, 2811, and 3825 routers. The attackers could then monitor all network communication and had the ability to infect other network devices. This vulnerability was brought into the network when a updated version of IOS was installed in the routers. Software updates seek to remain up to date and prevent vulnerability exploitation. Google's Project Zero is a great example of such practice. After discovering a number of vulnerabilities in various software used by end-users, Google formed a permanent team dedicated to finding software vulnerabilities.

1.4.2 Hardware vulnerabilities

Hardware vulnerabilities are often introduced by malfunctions in hardware design. For example, RAM memory is basically condensers installed very close to each other. It was found that constant changes applied to one of these condensers could affect neighbouring capacitors due to proximity. An exploit called Rowhammer was built on the basis of that design flaw. By more than once changing memory in similar locations, the Rowhammer misuse permits information to be recovered from close by address memory cells, regardless of whether the cells are secured. By repeatedly rewriting memory in the same addresses, the Rowhammer exploit allows data to be restored from nearby address memory cells, even if the cells are secured. Hardware vulnerabilities are unique to system models and usually are not exploited by attempts at random compromises. Although hardware vulnerabilities are more common in highly targeted attacks, standard malware protection and physical security are adequate everyday user protection. Malware Malicious software, or malware, is a piece of software that runs on the victims' computer without their knowledge or consent. It is often concealed in email attachments, software, websites, and other types of Trojan Horses. Trojan Horses is the term for a piece of software that is advertised as performing a certain task but executing other tasks in addition to its primary function. There are many reasons why people use this malicious software, including; Steal personal data like your bank account and credit card details Steal your companies data, records and intellectual property (IP) Use your computer in a botnet Extort money for removal and data recovery Disrupt IT systems and networks To cause havoc.

Chapter Two

2.1 What is Malware

Malware or malicious software is a document or code, normally conveyed over a system, that contaminates, investigates, takes or directs essentially any conduct an assailant needs. In spite of the fact that differed in type and abilities, malware for the most part has one of the accompanying targets:

a. Give remote control to an attacker to utilize a contaminated machine.
b. Send spam from the tainted machine to the clueless targets.
c. Examine the contaminated client's network activity

d. Steal sensitive information.

2.2 Types of Malware

Short for Malicious Software, malware is any code that can be used to steal data, bypass access controls, or cause harm to, or compromise a system. Below are a few common types of malware:

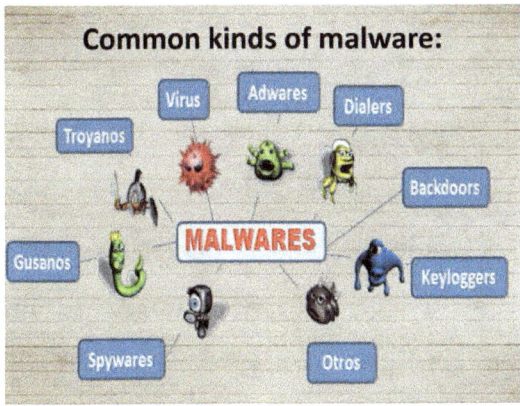

Figure 5: Common Types of Malware

2.2.1 Spyware

This malware is design to track and spy on the user. Spyware often includes activity trackers, keystroke collection, and data capture. In an attempt to overcome security measures, spyware often modifies security settings. Spyware often bundles itself with legitimate software or with Trojan horses.

2.2.2 Adware

Advertising supported software is designed to automatically deliver advertisements. Adware is often installed with some versions of software. Some adware is designed to only deliver advertisements but it is also common for adware to come with spyware.

2.2.3 Bot

From the word robot, a bot is malware designed to automatically perform action, usually online. While most bots are harmless, one increasing use of malicious bots is botnets. Several computers are infected with bots which are programmed to quietly wait for commands provided by the attacker.

2.2.4 Ransomware

This malware is designed to hold a computer system or the data it contains captive until a payment is made. Ransomware usually works by encrypting data in the computer with a key unknown to the user. Some other versions of ransomware can take advantage of specific system vulnerabilities to lock down the system. Ransomware is spread by a downloaded file or some software vulnerability.

2.2.5 Scareware

This is a type of malware designed to persuade the user to take a specific action based on fear. Scareware forges pop-up windows that resemble operating system dialogue windows. These windows convey forged messages stating the system is at risk or needs the execution of a specific program to return to normal operation. In reality, no problems were assessed or detected and if the user agrees and clears the mentioned program to execute, his or her system will be infected with malware.

2.2.6 Rootkit

This malware is designed to modify the operating system to create a backdoor. Attackers then use the backdoor to access the computer remotely. Most rootkits take advantage of software vulnerabilities to perform privilege escalation and modify system files. It is also common for rootkits to modify system forensics and monitoring tools, making them very hard to detect. Often, a computer infected by a rootkit must be wiped and reinstalled.

2.2.7 Virus

A virus is malicious executable code that is attached to other executable files, often legitimate programs. Most viruses require end-user activation and can activate at a specific time or date. Viruses can be harmless and simply display a picture or they can be destructive, such as those that modify or delete data. Viruses can also be programmed to mutate to avoid detection. Most viruses are now spread by USB drives, optical disks, network shares, or email.

2.2.8 Trojan horse

A Trojan horse is malware that carries out malicious operations under the guise of a desired operation. This malicious code exploits the privileges of the user that runs it. Often, Trojans are found in image files, audio files or games. A Trojan horse differs from a virus because it binds itself to non-executable files.

2.2.9 Worms

Worms are malicious code that replicates themselves by independently exploiting vulnerabilities in networks. Worms usually slow down networks. Whereas a virus requires a host program to run, worms can run by themselves. Other than the initial infection, they no longer require user participation. After a host is infected, the worm is able to spread very quickly over the network. Worms share similar patterns. They all have an enabling vulnerability, a way to propagate themselves, and they all contain a payload.

2.2.10 Man-In-The-Middle (MitM)

MitM allows the attacker to take control over a device without the user's knowledge. With that level of access, the attacker can intercept and capture user information before relaying it to its intended destination. MitM attacks are widely used to steal financial information. Many malware and techniques exist to provide attackers with MitM capabilities.

2.2.11 Man-In-The-Mobile (MitMo)

A variation of man-in-middle, MitMo is a type of attack used to take control over a mobile device. When infected, the mobile device can be instructed to exfiltrate user-sensitive information and send it to the attackers. ZeuS, an example of an exploit with MitMo capabilities, allows attackers quietly to capture 2-step verification SMS messages sent to users.

2.3 Symptoms of Malware

Regardless of the type of malware a system has been infected with, these are common malware symptoms: There is an increase in CPU usage. There is a decrease in computer speed. The computer freezes or crashes often. There is a decrease in Web browsing speed. There are unexplainable problems with network connections. Files are modified. Files are deleted. There is a presence of unknown files, programs, or desktop icons. There are unknown processes running. Programs are turning off or reconfiguring themselves. Email is being sent without the user's knowledge or consent.

2.4 How does your Malware infected your Computer

Malware can be infected your systems trough a various way, here are few common technique which attackers used to get the machine access.

Free Software

Free software is often bundled with other applications, often concealing their true purpose. These pose a great security risk and care should always be taken when installing new and often free software.

Bit Torrent

File sharing sites such as The Pirate Bay and uTorrent offer legal software and pirate movies to download. These files are shared many times and are easily infected with malware.

Hardware

Picked up a free USB memory stick from a trade show or borrowed one from a friend to transfer some files? Malware can be hidden in the firmware and is hard to detect.

Malicious Websites

Attackers often compromise or set up fake websites to download malware to visitors using the site. No user interaction is needed; the code is downloaded with the website data.

Social Engineering

Links and attachments from friends and school/college computers. These look like they are from a trusted source but often the users' computer or account has been compromised without their knowledge.

Chapter Three
3.1 Data privacy and protection

This chapter focuses on your personal devices and your personal data. It includes tips for protecting your devices, creating strong passwords and safely using wireless networks. It also discusses maintaining your data securely. Your online data is worth something to cyber criminals. This chapter briefly covers authentication techniques to help you maintain your data securely. It also covers ways to enhance the security of your online data with tips about what to do and what not to do online.

Figure 6: Data Protection Importance

3.1.1 Protect Your Computing Devices

Your computing devices store your data which contains numerous information of your daily life and activities on the internet and intranet. Below is a short list of steps you can take to protect your computing devices from intrusion

3.1.2 Keep the Firewall On

Whether it is a software firewall or a hardware firewall on a router, the firewall should be turned on and updated to prevent hackers from accessing your personal or company data. Click Windows 7 and 8.1 or Windows 10 to turn on the firewall in the respective version of Windows.

3.1.3 Use Antivirus software

Malicious software, such as viruses, Trojan horses, worms, ransomware and spyware, are installed on your computing devices without your permission, in order to gain access to your computer and your data. Viruses can destroy your data, slow down your computer, or take over your computer. One way viruses can take over your computer is by allowing spammers to broadcast emails using your account. Spyware can monitor your online activities, collect your personal information, or produce unwanted pop-up ads on your web browser while you are online. A good rule is to only download software from trusted websites to avoid getting spyware in the first place. Antivirus software is designed to scan your computer and incoming email for viruses and delete them. Sometimes antivirus software also includes antispyware. Keep your software up to date to protect your computer from the newest malicious software.

3.1.4 Managing OS and protecting devices

Your computing devices, whether they are PCs, laptops, tablets, or smart phones, should be password protected to prevent unauthorized access. The stored information should be encrypted, especially for sensitive or confidential data. For mobile devices, only store necessary information, in case these devices are stolen or lost when you are away from your home. If any one of your devices is compromised, the criminals may have access to all your data through your cloud-storage service provider, such as iCloud or Google drive. IoT devices pose an even greater risk than your other computing devices. While desktop, laptop and mobile platforms receive frequent software updates, most of the IoT devices still have their original firmware. If vulnerabilities are found in the firmware, the IoT device is likely to stay vulnerable. To make the problem worse, IoT devices are often designed to call home and require Internet access. To reach the Internet, most IoT devices manufacturers rely on the customer's local network. The result is that IoT devices are very likely to be comprised and when they are, they allow access to the customer's local network and data. The best way to protect you from this scenario is to have IoT devices using an isolated network, sharing it only with other IoT devices.

3.1.5 Wireless Networks Safely

Wireless networks allow Wi-Fi enabled devices, such as laptops and tablets, to connect to the network by way of the network identifier, known as the Service Set Identifier (SSID). To prevent intruders from entering your home wireless network, the pre-set SSID and default password for the browser-based administrative interface should be changed. Hackers will be aware of this kind of default access information. Optionally, the wireless router can also be configured to not broadcast the SSID, which adds an additional barrier to discovering the network. However, this should not be considered adequate security for a wireless network. Furthermore, you should encrypt wireless communication by enabling wireless security and the WPA2 encryption feature on the wireless router. Even with WPA2 encryption enabled, the wireless network can still be vulnerable. In

October 2017, a security flaw in the WPA2 protocol was discovered. This flaw allows an intruder to break the encryption between the wireless router and the wireless client, and allow the intruder to access and manipulate the network traffic.

This vulnerability can be exploited using **Key Reinstallation Attacks** (KRACK). It affects all modern, protected Wi-Fi networks. To mitigate an attacker, a user should update all affected products: wireless routers and any wireless capable devices, such as laptops and mobile devices, as soon as security updates become available. For laptops or other devices with wired NIC, a wired connection could mitigate this vulnerability. Furthermore, you can also use a trusted VPN service to prevent the unauthorized access to your data while you are using the wireless network. When you are away from home, a public Wi-Fi hot spot allows you to access your online information and surf the Internet. However, it is best to not access or send any sensitive personal information over a public wireless network. Verify whether your computer is configured with file and media sharing and that it requires user authentication with encryption. To prevent someone from intercepting your information (known as "eavesdropping") while using a public wireless network, use encrypted VPN tunnels and services. The VPN service provides you secure access to the

Internet, with an encrypted connection between your computer and the VPN service provider's VPN server. With an encrypted VPN tunnel, even if a data transmission is intercepted, it is not decipherable. Many mobile devices, such as smart phones and tablets, come with the Bluetooth wireless protocol. This capability allows Bluetooth-enabled devices to connect to each other and share information. Unfortunately, Bluetooth can be exploited by hackers to eavesdrop on some devices, establish remote access controls, distribute malware, and drain batteries. To avoid these issues, keep Bluetooth turned off when you are not using it.

Chapter Four

4.1 Social Engineering

Sometimes, the easiest way to obtain information is to deceive or trick someone to give you the information without the use of any technical hacking techniques. Social engineering is an access attack that attempts to manipulate individuals into performing actions or divulging confidential information.

Social engineers often rely on people's willingness to be helpful but also prey on people's weaknesses. For example, an attacker could call an authorized employee with an urgent problem that requires immediate network access. The attacker could appeal to the employee's vanity, invoke authority using name-dropping techniques, or appeal to the employee's greed.

Figure 7: Social Engineering Icon

Social engineering relies on exploiting human nature and trust. For example, a criminal might call reception claiming to be from the IT department and try to trick them to divulge information. In more sophisticated social engineering attempts, criminals have impersonated employees at a large corporation complete with a company logo shirt and used employee information gained on social media sites to gain access. Here discussed some techniques by the attackers which used for social engineering access.

4.1.1 Social Engineering Calls

You might receive a call from someone posing as a fellow employee from a different department or a contractor that needs access to the computer system.

4.1.2 In-Person

A new employee who hasn't been issued with their swipe card yet asking someone to hold the door for them. A strange person in the smoking area listening in to the office chat. The office WiFi password on a whiteboard for visitors to see. This scenario is In-Person engineering.

4.1.3 Online

Social networking sites such as LinkedIn make getting employee information very easy. A criminal can quickly put together detailed information that could be used in an attack.

4.2 Common Attacks techniques

There are many attacking techniques are being used by the attackers. Here below discussed about few of them which are mostly common techniques.

4.2.1 Pretexting

This is when an attacker calls an individual and lies to them in an attempt to gain access to privileged data. An example involves an attacker who pretends to need personal or financial data in order to confirm the identity of the recipient.

4.2.2 Tailgating

This is when an attacker quickly follows an authorized person into a secure location. Tailgating is often used by criminals who take benefits of a helpful employee or student holding a door open for someone such as a visitor without an identity, or someone in a dress appearing to be an employee.

4.2.3 Something for Something (Quid pro quo)

This is when an attacker requests personal information from a party in exchange for something, like a free gift. Many victim took this offer without even knowing that someone is taking their personal information without their consent.

4.2.4 Wifi Password Cracking

Wi-Fi password cracking is the process of discovering the password used to protect a wireless network. These are some techniques used in password cracking:

4.2.5 Social Engineering

The attacker manipulates a person who knows the password into providing it. Social engineers often rely on people's willingness to be helpful but also prey on people's weaknesses.

4.2.6 Brute-force attacks

The attacker tries several possible passwords in an attempt to guess the password. If the password is a 4-digit number, for example, the attacker would have to try every one of the 10000 combinations. Brute-force attacks usually involve a word-list file. This is a text file containing a list of words taken from a dictionary. A program then tries each word and common combinations. Because brute-force attacks take time, complex passwords take much longer to guess. A few password brute-force tools include Ophcrack, L0phtCrack, THC Hydra, RainbowCrack, and Medusa.

4.2.7 Network sniffing

By listening and capturing packets sent on the network, an attacker may be able to discover the password if the password is being sent unencrypted (in plain text). If the password is encrypted, the attacker may still be able to reveal it by using a password cracking tool.

4.2.8 **Phishing**

Phishing is when a malicious party sends a fraudulent email disguised as being from a legitimate, trusted source. The message intent is to trick the recipient into installing malware on their device, or into sharing personal or financial information. An example of phishing is an email forged to look like it was sent by a retail store asking the user to click a link to claim a prize. The link may go to a fake site asking for personal information, or it may install a virus. While phishing and spear phishing both use emails to reach the victims, spear phishing emails are customized to a specific person. The attacker researches the target's interests before sending the email. For example, an attacker learns the target is interested in cars, and has been looking to buy a specific model of car. The attacker joins the same car discussion forum where the target is a member, forges a car sale offering and sends email to the target. The email contains a link for pictures of the car. When targeted click on the link the victim computer has been compromised.

4.2.9 DDoS

A Distributed DoS Attack (DDoS) is similar to a DoS attack but originates from multiple, coordinated sources. As an example, a DDoS attack could proceed as follows: An attacker builds a network of infected hosts, called a botnet. The infected hosts are called zombies. The zombies are controlled by handler systems. The zombie computers constantly scan and infect more hosts, creating more zombies. When ready, the hacker instructs handler systems to make the botnet of zombies carry out a DDoS attack.

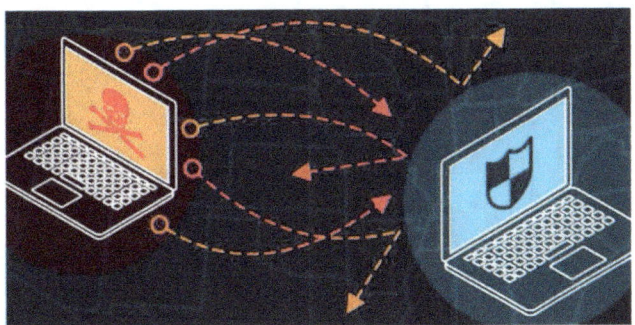

Figure 8: DDoS attack

4.2.10 SEO Poisoning

Search engines such as Google work by ranking pages and presenting relevant results based on users' search queries. Depending on the relevancy of web site content, it may appear higher or lower in the search result list. SEO, short for Search Engine Optimization, is a set of techniques used to improve a website's ranking by a search engine. While many legitimate companies specialize in optimizing websites to better position them, a malicious user could use SEO to make a malicious website appear higher in search results. This technique is called SEO poisoning. The most common goal of SEO poisoning is to increase traffic to malicious sites that may host malware or perform social engineering.

Figure 9: SEO Poisoning

4.3 What is Impact Reduction

While the majority of successful companies today are aware of common security issues and put considerable effort towards preventing them, no set of security practices is 100% efficient. Because a breach is likely to happen if the prize is big, companies and organizations must also be prepared to contain the damage. It is important to understand that the impact of a breach is not only related to the technical aspect of it, stolen data, damaged databases, or damage to intellectual property, the damage also extends to the company's reputation. Responding to a data breach is a very dynamic process. Below are some important measures a company should take when a security breach is identified, according to many security experts: Communicate the issue. Internally employees should be informed of the problem and called to action. Externally, clients should be informed through direct communication and official announcements. Communication creates transparency, which is crucial in this type of situation. Be sincere and accountable in case the company is at fault. Provide details. Explain why the situation took place and what was compromised. It is also expected that the company take care of the costs of identity theft protection services for affected customers. Understand what caused and facilitated the breach. If necessary, hire forensics experts to research and learn the details. Apply what was learned from the forensics investigation to ensure similar breaches do not happen in the future. Ensure all systems are clean, no backdoors were installed, and nothing else has been compromised. Attackers will often attempt to leave a backdoor to facilitate future breaches. Make sure this does not happen. Educate employees, partners and increase awareness.

4.4 How to Prevent Social Engineering

The most effective measure that you or an organization can take against social engineering is regular training. User awareness of the threats and techniques used is essential to help you spot suspicious activity. Limit personal information on social media sites. Additional security policies and procedures that outline how employees deal with calls and requests for information. Review and audit user training and procedures. Following some basic guidelines will help you stay safe and secure.

4.4.1 Keep software and your computer system updated

Software companies release updates to patch any security issues that have been found. Malware will search for outdated software to take advantage of any vulnerability that hasn't been patched.

4.4.2 Think twice before clicking on links

Always be suspicious of links even if they are sent by friends or companies that are known to you. Most of the times unknown sender email links detected as spam so don't put them back into your inbox unless you are sure about the mail content.

4.4.3 Don't trust free software

Try and use software by trusty companies and stay away from free software found on the internet. Most of the time free software contains viruses and adware which may harm your computer or even you may trap into a ransom ware. A simple example, sometimes you used performance boost or disk cleaning application to speed up your computer performance. What happened here, that software developer inbuilt many free adware or even virus into that program so when you launch that application it can directly run into your computer and damage your hard disc or passes your precious information into a tunnel where attacker listening.

4.4.4 Back up your data

Make a copy of the important data and files and your computer and store it in a safe place. This will protect you from ransom ware and will make it easier if you need to restore your system at a later date.

4.4.5 Use security software

Good security software will protect your computer from being compromised and block any suspicious activity. Upgrade your antivirus or security definition regularly so it can detect new viruses and storms.

4.4.6 Protecting your computing devices

Your computing devices store your data and are the portal to your online life. Below is a short list of steps you can take to protect your computing devices from intrusion:

4.4.7 Firewall Manage

Whether it is a software firewall or a hardware firewall on a router, the firewall should be turned on and updated to prevent hackers from accessing your personal or company data.

4.4.8 Use Antivirus and Antispyware

Malicious software, such as viruses, Trojan horses, worms, ransom ware and spyware, are installed on your computing devices without your permission, in order to gain access to your computer and your data. Viruses can destroy your data, slow down your computer, or take over your computer. One way viruses can take over your computer is by allowing spammers to broadcast emails using your account. Spyware can monitor your online activities, collect your personal information, or produce unwanted pop-up ads on your web browser while you are online. A good rule is to only download software from trusted websites to avoid getting spyware in the first place. Antivirus software is designed to scan your computer and incoming email for viruses and delete them. Sometimes antivirus software also includes antispyware. Keep your software up to date to protect your computer from the newest malicious software.

4.4.9 Manage Your Operating System and Browser

Hackers are always trying to take advantage of vulnerabilities in your operating systems and your web browsers. To protect your computer and your data, set the security settings on your computer and browser at medium or higher. Update your computer's operating system including your web browsers and regularly download and install the latest software patches and security updates from the vendors.

4.4.10 Protect All Your Devices

Your computing devices, whether they are PCs, laptops, tablets, or smart phones, should be password protected to prevent unauthorized access. The stored information should be encrypted, especially for sensitive or confidential data. For mobile devices, only store necessary information, in case these devices are stolen or lost when you are away from your home. If any one of your devices is compromised, the criminals may have access to all your data through your cloud-storage service provider, such as iCloud or Google drive. IoT devices pose an even greater risk than your other computing devices. While desktop, laptop and mobile platforms receive frequent software updates, most of the IoT devices still have their original firmware. If vulnerabilities are found in the firmware, the IoT device is likely to stay vulnerable. To make the problem worse, IoT devices are often designed to call home and require Internet access. To reach the Internet, most IoT devices manufacturers rely on the customer's local network. The result is that IoT devices are very likely to be comprised and when they are, they allow access to the customer's local network and data. The best way to protect you from this scenario is to have IoT devices using an isolated network, sharing it only with other IoT devices.

4.4.11 Use unique passwords for each account

You probably have more than one online account, and each account should have a unique password. That is a lot of passwords to remember. However, the consequence of not using strong and unique passwords leaves you and your data vulnerable to cyber criminals. Using the same password for all your online accounts is like using the same key for all your locked doors, if an attacker was to get your key, he would have the ability to access everything you own. If criminals get your password through phishing for example, they will try to get into your other online accounts. If you only use one password for all accounts, they can get into all your accounts, steal or erase all your data, or decide to impersonate you. We use so many online accounts that need passwords that is becomes too much to remember. One solution to avoid reusing passwords or using weak passwords is to use a password manager. A password manager stores and encrypts all of your different and complex passwords. The manager can then help you to log into your online accounts automatically. You only need to remember your master password to access the password manager and manage all of your accounts and passwords.

4.4.12 Tips for choosing a good password

Do not use dictionary words or names in any languages Do not use common misspellings of dictionary words Do not use computer names or account names If possible use special characters, such as ! @ # $ % ^ & * ( ) Use a password with ten or more characters

4.4.13 Encrypt your Data

Your data should always be encrypted. You may think you have no secrets and nothing to hide so why use encryption? Maybe you think that nobody wants your data. Most likely, this is probably not true. Are you ready to show all of your photos and documents to strangers? Are you ready to share financial information stored on your computer to your friends? Do you want to give out your emails and account passwords to the general public? This can be even more troublesome if a malicious application infects your computer or mobile device and steals potentially valuable information, such as account numbers and passwords, and other official documents. That kind of information can lead to identity theft, fraud, or ransom. Criminals may decide to simply encrypt your data and make it unusable until you pay the ransom. What is encryption? Encryption is the process of converting the information into a form where an unauthorized party cannot read it. Only a trusted, authorized person with the secret key or password can decrypt the data and access it in its original form. The encryption itself does not prevent someone from intercepting the data. Encryption can only prevent an unauthorized person from viewing or accessing the content. Software programs are used to encrypt files, folders, and even entire drives. Encrypting File System (EFS) is a Windows feature that can encrypt data. EFS is directly linked to a specific user account. Only the user that encrypted the data will be able to access it after it has been encrypted using EFS.

4.4.14 Social Media Sharing

If you want to keep your privacy on the social media, share as little information as possible. You should not share information like your birth date, email address, or your phone number on your profile. The people who need to know your personal information probably already know it. Do not fill out your social media profile completely; only provide the minimum required information. Furthermore, check your social media settings to allow only people you know to see your activities or engage in your conversations. The more personal information you share online, the easier it is for someone to create a profile about you and take advantage of you offline. Have you ever forgotten the username and password for an online account? Security questions like "What is your mother's maiden name?" or "In what city were you born?" are supposed to help keep your account safe from intruders. However, anyone who wants to access your accounts can search for the answers on the Internet. You can answer these questions with false information, as long as you can remember the false answers. If you have a problem remembering them, you can use password manager to manage them for you.

4.4.15 Phishing Emails and Calls

Phishing emails are an attempt by scammers to trick you into giving out personal details such as bank account information, username, and passwords through fake emails. A scammer contacts you pretending to be from a legitimate business such as your bank, internet service provider, or other trusted companies. You may be contacted by email or increasingly by phone. The scammer asks you to provide or confirm your personal details. For example, the scammer may say that the bank or organization is verifying customer records to process a refund to your account. Or, they may ask you to fill out a customer survey and offer a prize for participating. Alternatively, the scammer may alert you to 'unauthorized or suspicious activity on your account'. You might be told that a large purchase has been made in a foreign country and asked if you authorized the payment. If you reply that you didn't, the scammer will ask you to confirm your credit card or bank details so the 'bank' can investigate. In some cases, the scammer may already have your credit card number and ask you to confirm your identity by quoting the 3 or 4 digit security code printed on the card. Phishing email messages are designed to look genuine, and often copy the format used by the organization the scammer is pretending to represent, including their branding and logo. They may take you to a fake website that looks like the real deal but has a slightly different address. For example, if the legitimate site is 'www.yourbank.com', the scammer may use an address like 'www.yourbnk.com'. If you provide the scammer with your details online or over the phone, they will use them to carry out fraudulent activities, such as using your credit cards and stealing your money.

Can you spot the signs of a Phishing email?   5.1 Warning Signs
the email or message does not address you by your proper name. Scammers will send out thousands of emails and will use an initial greeting like "Dear Customer" or "Dear <your email address>". There may be typing errors and grammatical mistakes within the email. The "from" address will not look correct. Any website links do not look like the address you usually use and are requesting details the legitimate site does not normally ask for. The message will often require you to take urgent action. Be careful of emails containing phrases like "your account will be closed," "your account has been compromised," or "urgent action required".

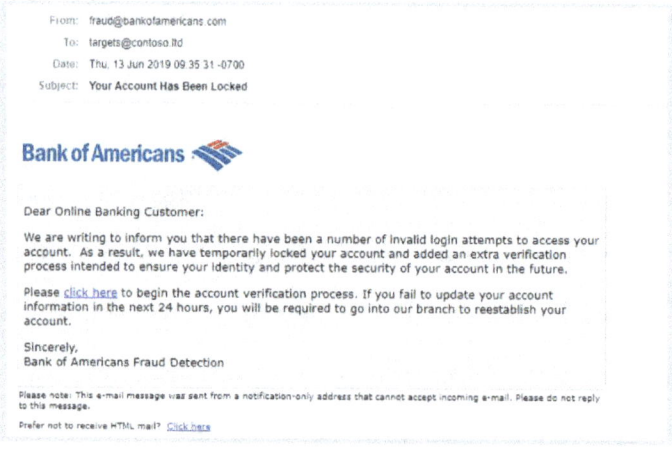

Figure 10: Phishing email sample

4.5 Email and Web Browser Privacy

Every day, millions of email messages are used to communicate with friends and conduct business. Email is a convenient way to communicate with each other quickly. When you send an email, it is similar to sending a message using a postcard. The postcard message is transmitted in plain sight of anyone who has access to look, and the email message is transmitted in plain text, and is readable by anyone who has access. These communications are also passed among different servers while in route to the destination. Even when you erase your email messages, the messages can be archived on the mail servers for some time. Anyone with physical access to your computer, or your router, can view which websites you have visited using web browser history, cache, and possibly log files. This problem can be minimized by enabling the in-private browsing mode on the web browser. Most of the popular web browsers have their own name for private browser mode: Microsoft Internet Explorer: In Private Google Chrome: Incognito Mozilla Firefox: Private tab / private window Safari: Private: Private browsing With private mode enabled, cookies are disabled, and temporary Internet files and browsing history are removed after closing the window or program. Keeping your Internet browsing history private may prevent others from gathering information about your online activities and enticing you to buy something with targeted ads. Even with private browsing enabled and cookies disabled, companies are developing different ways of fingerprinting users in order to gather information and track user behaviour. For example, the intermediary devices, such as routers, can have information about a user's web surfing history. Ultimately, it is your responsibility to safeguard your data, your identity, and your computing devices. When you send an email, should you include your medical records? The next time you browse the Internet, is your transmission secure? Just a few simple precautions may save you problems later.

4.6 Security Best Practices

Many national and professional organizations have published lists of security best practices. The following is a list of some security best practices:

a. Perform Risk Assessment

Knowing the value of what you are protecting will help in justifying security expenditures.

b. **Create a Security Policy**

Create a policy that clearly outlines company rules, job duties, and expectations.

c. **Physical Security Measures**

Restrict access to networking closets, server locations, as well as fire suppression.

d. **Human Resource Security Measures**

Employees should be properly researched with background checks

e. **Perform and Test Backups**

Perform regular backups and test data recovery from backups.

f. **Maintain Security Patches and Updates**

Regularly update server, client, and network device operating systems and programs.

g. **Employ Access Controls**

Configure user roles and privilege levels as well as strong user authentication.

h. **Regularly Test Incident Response**

Employ an incident response team and test emergency response scenarios.

i. **Implement a Network Monitoring, Analytics and Management Tool**

Implement Network Security devices use next generation routers, firewalls, and other security appliances. Use enterprise level antimalware and antivirus software.

j. **Educate Users**

Educate users and employees in secure procedures. Conduct training to existing and newly appointed staffs about the internet and intranet securities.

k. **Encrypt data**

Encrypt all sensitive company data including email. Some of the most helpful guidelines are found in organizational repositories such as the National Institute of Standards and Technology (NIST) Computer Security Resource Centre, as shown in the figure. One of the most widely known and respected organizations for cyber security training is the SANS Institute.

4.7 IDS and IPS

An Intrusion Detection System (IDS), shown in the figure, is either a dedicated network device, or one of several tools in a server or firewall that scans data against a database of rules or attack signatures, looking for malicious traffic. If a match is detected, the IDS will log the detection, and create an alert for a network administrator. The Intrusion Detection System does not take action when a match is detected so it does not prevent attacks from happening. The job of the IDS is merely to detect, log and report. The scanning performed by the IDS slows down the network (known as latency). To prevent against network delay, an IDS is usually placed offline, separate from regular network traffic. Data is copied or mirrored by a switch and then forwarded to the IDS for offline detection. There are also IDS tools that can be installed on top of a host computer operating system, like Linux or Windows. An Intrusion Prevention System (IPS) has the ability to block or deny traffic based on a positive rule or signature match. One of the most well-known IPS/IDS systems is Snort. The commercial version of Snort is Cisco's Source fire. Source fire has the ability to perform real-time traffic and port analysis, logging, content searching and matching, and can detect probes, attacks, and port scans. It also integrates with other third party tools for reporting, performance and log analysis.

4.8 Mobile or Cell Phone Security so what could happen?

If you lose you're Smartphone or it is stolen: It could be used to access your bank account or steal your identity using information stored on your device. You may lose irreplaceable data like photos, videos, and messages. Your social media accounts could be accessed, which could enable someone to pose as you or steal your identity. Someone could use your phone to make fraudulent phone calls on your account. You may have to cover the cost of a new device while still paying off the lost or stolen one.

Protect yourself by securing your phone Use the following advice to make your Smartphone more secure: Set a password, Personal Identification Number (PIN), pass code, gesture, or fingerprint that must be entered to unlock the device. Don't forget to put PINs on your SIM card and voicemail, and ensure your device is set to automatically lock. Install reputable security software that includes antivirus and anti-theft/loss protection. Only install applications from the official device application store and do not modify or 'jailbreak' your device.

Figure 11 : Phone Security Steps

Use your device's automatic update feature to install new application and operating system updates as soon as they are available. Set the device to require a password before applications are installed. This will prevent unauthorized modifications to the device. Leave Bluetooth turned off or in undiscoverable (hidden) mode when you are not using it. Ensure your device does not automatically connect to new networks without your permission. Enable the remote locking and/or wiping functions, if your phone is lost or stolen.

Chapter Five

5.1 Contingency Plan

A security breach occurs when someone gains unauthorized access to your IT systems and data. Cybercriminals or malicious applications bypass security mechanisms to reach restricted areas. Whether you are an individual or part of an organization, a contingency plan needs to be developed. It will assist with data and systems being recovered quickly and effectively following a service disruption or disaster. A contingency plan is a course of action designed to help an organization respond effectively to a significant future event or situation.

Figure 12: Contingency Plan

5.2 IT contingency planning

This is a vital component of business continuity, disaster recovery, and risk management. It may also cover other aspects of your IT infrastructure risks: equipment failure malware data loss theft cybercrime human error keeping accurate network diagrams will assist in disaster recovery.

Figure 13: Business Contingency Example

The contingency plan and processes should highlight specific considerations and concerns associated with planning for various types of IT systems and provide examples to assist users in developing their own IT contingency plans. It should consider: Business impact analysis roles and responsibilities identify critical

Risks preventative controls reporting and notification keeping logs damage assessment backup methods plan activation contingency solutions recovery procedures.

5.3 **Virtual Private Network (VPN)**

One is the most common methods to protect your network data is the use of a Virtual Private Network (VPN). A VPN encrypts all the data that is transmitted between the remote device (computer, Smartphone, etc.) and the destination over an insecure network like the internet. You can use a VPN to connect to your office, home, or school and your data will be encapsulated within a secure tunnel. VPN software is relatively inexpensive and easy to set up, it's often included in anti-virus and security software from companies like Norton, Avast, and AVG.

Cyber security best practices it's easy to believe that because you have a small business or work alone that cyber criminals will not be interested in attacking your company. The "not much to steal" mindset is common with small business owners in regards to cyber security, but it is also completely incorrect and out of sync with today's cyber security best practices. Use strong passwords and authentication Install security software like anti-malware and firewalls document your cyber security policy make a contingency plan regularly back up your data train and educate yourself and others be aware of suspicious links and emails physically secure your IT equipment use a VPN if you are remote working keep operating systems and software updated.

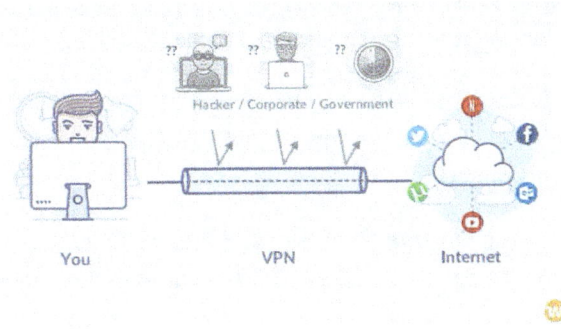

Figure 14: VPN Network

5.4 Concluding Speech

A cyber attack contingency plan is a recommendation that companies ought to decide whether to prevent cyber attacks. Cyber-attacks produce disclosure of information, erasure, unavailability of hard drives and facilities. There are multiple potential variables considered in the best contingency plan due to Informatics or human failure. The workers of the company need the encouragement to take good care of data through the promotions of obligations and loyalties.

References

CISA. (2009, Oct 22). *Avoid Social Engineering Attack*. Retrieved Nov 10, 2020, from CISA: https://us-cert.cisa.gov/ncas/tips/ST04-014

CISCO. (2018, Nov 10). *How to protect Malware*. Retrieved Nov 20, 2020, from Protecting Malware: https://www.cisco.com/c/en/us/products/security/advanced-malware-protection/what-is-malware.html#~how-malware-works

Duey, S. (n.d.). *Reducing Risk*. Retrieved November 01, 2020, from Cybersecurity Magazine: https://www.uscybersecurity.net/why-trojans-and-malware-are-targeting-college-students/

Fruhlinger, J. (n.d.). *The CIA Triad*. Retrieved October 21, 2020, from CSO Online: https://www.csoonline.com/article/3519908/the-cia-triad-definition-components-and-examples.html

Glossary. (2015, Jan 10). *European Union Agency for Cyberseucity*. Retrieved Nov 20, 2020, from European Union Agency for Cyberseucity: https://www.enisa.europa.eu/topics/csirts-in-europe/glossary/man-in-the-middle

Harmening, J. (2009). In J. H. Joe Wright, *Computer & Information Security Handbook* (p. 928). New York: Elsevier Inc.

Md Tapon Mahamud Jony, 2020, Cybersecurity Defense, INTERNATIONAL JOURNAL OF ENGINEERING RESEARCH & TECHNOLOGY (IJERT) Volume 09, Issue 12 (December 2020),

PaloAlto. (2019, Jan 19). *Palo Alto Networks*. Retrieved July 10, 2020, from What is malware: https://www.paloaltonetworks.com/cyberpedia/what-is-malware

Rountree, D. (2011). In D. Rountree, *Security for Microsoft Windows System Administrators* (pp. 210-220). New York: Elsevier Inc.

Swanson, M. M. (2002, 06 13). *NIST*. Retrieved Nov 6th, 2020, from https://www.nist.gov/publications/contingency-planning-guide-information-technology-systems#:~:text=Contingency%20planning%20refers%20to%20interim,IT%20functions%20using%20manual%20methods.

SWG. (2020, Nov 20). Retrieved Nov 20, 2020, from Security: https://swgfl.org.uk/security/types-of-malware/

Thomson Reuters. (2015, Sept 16). *CBC*. Retrieved Aug 19, 2020, from Technology and Science: https://www.cbc.ca/news/technology/synful-knock-router-malware-1.3228732

Types of Malware. (n.d.). Retrieved 10 20, 2020, from https://swgfl.org.uk/security/types-of-malware/

UK Governance. (2010, Nov 20). *What is social engineering*. Retrieved Oct 15, 2020, from IT Governance: https://www.itgovernance.co.uk/social-engineering-attacks

Vladimir Sanchez Padilla 1, F. F. (2019). A Contingency Plan Framework for Cyber-Attacks. *Journal of Information Systems Engineering & Management*, 5-6.

Wikipedia. (n.d.). *Information Security*. Retrieved Aug 21, 2020, from Wiki: https://en.wikipedia.org/wiki/Information_security

END